AMERICA
THE BEAUTIFUL HAS
PROBLEMS

Charleston, SC
www.PalmettoPublishing.com

America The Beautiful Has Problems

Copyright © 2023 by William Lawrence Drake

All rights reserved

First Edition

Hardcover ISBN: 979-8-8229-2864-0
Paperback ISBN: 979-8-8229-2865-7
eBook ISBN: 979-8-8229-2866-4

AMERICA
THE BEAUTIFUL HAS
PROBLEMS

Divisions Between Conservatives,
Choosing Sides, Deciding Who's the Enemy

WILLIAM LAWRENCE DRAKE

TABLE OF CONTENTS

▲ ▲ ▲

AMERICA THE BEAUTIFUL
HAS PROBLEMS

▲ ▲ ▲

Division between conservatives and liberals, choosing sides, deciding who's the enemy.

For weeks it has been the author's intention not to get involved politically with what can be clearly seen as a DIVIDED AMERICA. As it stands right now, it is difficult to understand why this country has come to a point where Americans are forced to choose between the destruction of America, and Equal Justice.

Not since the Civil War, segregation, and The Civil Rights era, has this nation been locked in a senseless debate about who is RIGHT or WRONG, who is conservative or liberal, or wasting time ATTEMPTING to determine who the Enemy is politically – When we examine or seek answers as to why this debate is necessary, WE FIND THAT THE ANSWER IS NOT FOUND IN OTHERS, BUT WITHIN OURSELVES - In other words, the true enemy is us!

As Americans, it is very important that we remember to forgive those who act, or oppose us in their thinking, or that have intentions to destroy this nation instead of building a better America. GOD said: "For your thoughts are not my thoughts, neither are your ways

1

my ways," declared the Lord. "As the heavens are higher than the earth, so are my ways higher than your ways and my thoughts than your thoughts." ... ISAIAH 55 8-9

America has a responsibility for strong believers in God to: (1) stay the course, (2) stand tall in spirit, and (3) give all that they must to save this great nation from harm and defeat. Unlike other countries, America must take a step back from where this country stands today, DIVIDED, and begin to think about UNITY in purpose, which means learning to disagree without becoming disagreeable, loving each other, as GOD loved us, and being patient listeners to avoid divisive debate.

JOSHUA 1–8: says to us "BE STRONG and COURAGEOUS", and NEHEMIAH lays before us a plan to build a better America, and the World, the book says:

1. Don't be distracted.
2. Follow the plan set before you.
3. When opposition comes, stay focused.
4. Safeguard your goals, be selective about sharing.
5. Evaluate your critics, to determine where they are with respect to your purpose.
6. Assess your critics in terms of their ability, or lack thereof!
7. Don't discuss your concerns – to discuss a problem/concern with an idiot, MAKES YOU AN IDIOT!
8. Follow God in whatever HE Plans, and the plan will work.

America's direction and political leadership, cannot and will not show other countries the positive aspects of Democracy if we continue to be a divided nation – Presently, Democracy gives an appearance of justice denied; instead of what justice should be in America - justice has become who do you know, and WHAT POSITION

YOU HOLD - Distractions such as, requiring every American to purchase an electric vehicle, or taking general household products out of homes, are used to keep power in the hands of POLITICAL PARTIES so that divisions of class and race, can persists to: (1) create sound bites for media, and (2) take focus away from more important issues, e.g., the border, inflation, crime, and a failing education system!

FOR ADULTS ONLY: Argument about data, information that cannot be proven (Climate Change), and unfounded theory about America's future are unending, and unwinnable; therefore, spending time, energy, and effort on these issues is fruitless. AMERICANS must take back control of OUR AMERICA, not by force, riots, or war, but with COMMON SENSE. Above all else, America must return to the guiding principles that were established by this NATION in 1776.

"In 1776, America's Founders gathered in Philadelphia to draft the Declaration of Independence, which dissolved the political ties that had bound the American people to Great Britain. A new nation was thus born, free and independent, the United States of America."

For the record, no one should be influenced by polls or politicians, as polls and politicians do not repair, or fix problems, they seemingly make problems worse. Politicians should be elected because of their willingness to help people that have lost their way in life because of DRUGS, GANGS, and CRIME, to include others that have lost their belief in the American way of life – And the government, Institutions, and organizations, have been contaminated with a disease that is designed to eliminate God from public platforms.

The government is making policy/rules to cancel Christian's voices; while at the same time giving LOUD VOICES to activist which supports gender transition, crime, and dependence on a government that causes inner-city voters to vote against their interest in return for small amounts of money!

The Bible, the Declaration of Independence, the Constitution of the United States, Robert's Rules of Order, have become meaningless because authority has been delegated to others that desire to keep uneducated voters voting for politicians that keep chaos, and racial division in place to be re-elected! When these politicians are re-elected, they hire security to protect themselves from the very people that voted for them, the poor!

America the beautiful has problems, and if these problems are not corrected, America will not represent, or be, the "Home of the Brave" or "land of the free." How did WE get to this point? And why are WE not doing anything to get on the right track? Given the dangers that America faces, why aren't politicians focusing on the crime problem, OUR immigrant problem, and OUR spending problem? According to history, ALL GREAT CIVILIZATIONS FAILED because of internal strife, and leaders that were self-centered and EVIL!

AMERICA IS IN DANGER

▲ ▲ ▲

America, as a country/nation, MUST RETURN to a time in history where patriotism, and the painstakingly articulated efforts of OUR FOUNDING FATHERS masterfully created THE DECLARATION OF INDEPENDENCE, and THE CONSTITUTION OF THE UNITED STATES OF AMERICA - This nation must go back to a time when GOD was important and included in our daily operations; God was also included in our public schools, the Pledge of Allegiance WAS LEARNED AND SAID EACH MORNING by students, and America the beautiful, was indeed a beautiful place to live!

Rick Warren, the author of THE PURPOSE DRIVEN LIFE, WROTE: "How you relate to God on earth will determine where you spend eternity. If you develop a relationship of love and trust in God through His Son Jesus Christ, you'll spend the rest of eternity with him…"

But it is important to recognize, that Americans must avoid DISTRACTIONS, to include politicians who lie to constituents or conflate the truth with illogical data - parents must take charge of their families and teach their children that gender is not decided after birth. Adults must teach others, who are younger, that" hope springs eternal," and that God is alive!

The danger to America is alive in divisiveness: republican's vs democrats, racial divisions, the have's vs the have-nots, but more than these visible divisions is that OUR government appears to profit from and instigate divisions. Lord Acton, said: "Power corrupts, and Absolute Power Corrupts absolutely!" When States are granted absolute power, a monster has been created, and it lives among us!

America in 2023 is facing new challenges as OUR divided country continues down a path of revenge, hate and a lack of trust – The negative paths that America travels will consume this nation in the same way that THE BIBLE explains why God caused the GREAT FLOOD; HE was angry because people were not following his instructions - and as our history records The Rise and Fall of Rome, The Rise and Fall of Germany, Japan, and Rome for the second time, it should be recognized that God is watching us today.

America is now being challenged by our elected US Government to remove Fossil Fuels, Air Conditions, and Gas Stoves – Additionally, the government uses policy/mandates to force Americans to drive Electric Vehicles, Use Digital Currency, Allow the Borders to act as sieves, Defund the Police; and REMOVE GOD, along with HISTORY, from all public platforms!

FOR ADULTS ONLY: Understand that these comments are not about the criticism of America, but instead are observations of a GOVERNMENT that is forcibly taking control of a NATION with policy and mandates; then assumes that the policy changes and mandates are the best way to govern. It also appears that OUR government is attempting to control the lives of citizens by taking away America's birthright, FREEDOM OF CHOICE!

CRIME AND CROWDS

▲ ▲ ▲

California, New York, Philadelphia, Chicago,
Missouri, Baltimore, and Ohio

Should citizens leave a state simply because crime has spiraled out-of-control, and what is accomplished by abandoning States with high crime problems? Statistically, crime is created by SINGLE PEOPLE WITH CHILDREN – single people with children, in many cases, are usually sponsored by Welfare Programs – Welfare recipients are found in INNER-CITIES - Children that grow up in single people with children type families do so in dysfunctional social environments. Dysfunctional social environments usually lead to anti-social behavior: Children that begin life in families with mothers who are heads-of-household, most often only care about self, their survival, or their desires!

In many circumstances, children that are unlucky enough to be born in a SINGLE PEOPLE WITH CHILDREN family, are not taught about God, or kindness, or love, or respect – And usually this untaught teaching about God, or respect for others, leads to an unfeeling child who practices what they have been taught, being cold-hearted, and amoral; their participation in violent acts when in a crowd of other young people becomes a certainty, and sooner-or-later, these children will explode!

In normal relationships, "BIRDS OF A FEATHER, WILL FLOCK TOGETHER" … Criminals are no different in terms of seeking friendships, acquaintances, and "ROAD DOGS" that have the same psychological makeups! When delinquent crowds are examined closely, it is easily recognized how the CYCLE OF POVERTY develops - some of the children that are found in CRIMINAL CROWDS, (crowds that consists of thugs, criminals, delinquents, or other misguided children), are sexually promiscuous - When these delinquents grow up, they become SINGLE PEOPLE WITH CHILDREN.

FOR ADULTS ONLY: Sexual activity is not an expression of FREEDOM – sexual experiences should be held to a higher standard than:" I HIT IT", or "KNOCKING BOOTS" - The Sexual experience should be AN ACT that is granted to MARRIED COUPLES ONLY! Yet many sexually active people believe that RAW DOG SEX (sex without condoms) is "DOING THEIR OWN THANG"! In the sixties, GETTING SOME, or HAVING SEX was the only way that boys could be called men! Girls were thought of as" FREAKS" by boys who thought they had become men when they had sex - UNFORTUNATELY, men of this era taught boys that becoming a man meant boys must have had sex to be called a man!

DON'T FORGET, boys were teased when it was discovered that they were virgins… AND SOME BOYS LIED TO AVOID BEING REDICULED for not having ENGAGED in a sexual experience! Basically, getting a girl pregnant was a major plus, and proved that a young man or a boy had become a man. Today, 2023, in inner-cities, getting girls pregnant, creates TROPHYIES, these newborns are taken care of by TAXPAYERS – In the sixties, a girl that got pregnant was embarrassed, WHICH USUALLY REQUIRED THE GIRL TO DROP-OUT-OF-SCHOOL, OR GET MARRIED.

Should one wonder why sexual behavior has been associated and/or linked with Crime and Crowds, let me announce that's why major cities are now facing crowds of young people who are taking advantage of DEFUND THE POLICE initiatives to steal from stores - **These same young people are more-than-likely the offspring of SINGLE PEOPLE WITH CHILDREN.**

Before you get angry at the author, lets again look at history - Going back to The Great Society, which was the brainchild of President Lyndon Banes Johnson, it is my opinion, that The Great Society, was/is the worst decision ever made by a Political Leader – as this Presidential decision allowed women to use taxpayer's support much like a husband! In essence, husbands were excused from their responsibilities – and most fathers of children never married the women/girls that they impregnated; and in many states**, should a female marry, she could not use taxpayer's funds to support the marriage – some states would not allow women/ girls to give birth to more than three (3) children at taxpayer expense – however, many states will not support a fourth child , BUT will FUND ABORTIONS.**

THE ABORTION DIVIDE, a Frontline and PBS video reveals, without mentioning the cost of abortions, how and why some women choose to have abortions. I will not judge or participate in condemning abortions, as I am not GOD, but I will state my opinion: I don't see that financing an abortion should become the responsibility of taxpayers. And I will ask the readers of this book to self-examine to determine if an abortion is biblical. PSALM 102: 18 states, "Write down for the coming generation what the LORD has done, So that people not yet born will praise him."

Rick Warren used scripture in the book of ISAIAH 44: 2 CEV which says, "I am your Creator, you were in my care even before you were born," says the LORD. This scripture accompanied a second scripture: PSALM 139: 16 LB, and it reads: "O Lord, You saw me before I was born and scheduled each day of my life before I began to breathe. Every day was recorded in your book!"

Each person must decide how to evaluate abortion for their purposes, as was voiced in my opinion, so too should everyone determine what their position will be about abortion – Again, let me reiterate that it is not the purpose of this book to change minds, or to influence each reader to think about abortion(s) the same way as is written in this manuscript.

However, it is essential that the great minds of America meet to discuss, not argue about abortion. The time is now when all Americans must look at abortion(s) to determine where THEY stand with respect to the topic of abortion.

CRIME IN AMERICA

▲ ▲ ▲

2 PETER: 5-7 In summary introduces, VIRTURE, KNOWLEDGE, TEMPERANCE, PATIENCE, GODLINESS, BROTHERLY KINDNESS, and CHARITY.

2 PETER: 8-9, says, "If these things be in you, and abound they make you that ye shall neither be barren nor unfruitful in the knowledge of our Lord Jesus Christ...But he that lacketh these things is blind and cannot see afar off, and hath forgotten that he was purged from his old sins."

Crime has two distinct characteristics: crimes against persons, and crimes against property – Crimes, such as fraud, are not verbally mentioned as a crime, but should be! Violent crimes are crimes that are largely forbidden because of the manner and style of the offenses that are committed: to take one's life or property requires force – force is classified as a weapon or size that is used to effectuate or complete a crime.

Fraud, although not mentioned as a real offense, represents crimes that are committed by SMART PEOPLE, but is none-the-less a crime. Webster's New World Dictionary defines fraud/fraudulent as: 1.a) deceit; trickery; cheating b) intentional deception to cause a person to give up property or some lawful right. 2. Something said or done to deceive; trick; artifice. 3.a person who deceives or is not what he pretends to be; imposter; cheat.

Fraudulent, 1. Acting with fraud; deceitful 2. based on or characterized by fraud 3. Done or obtained by fraud.

Crimes are invasive, cruel, and dangerous! But more than this, crimes separate families, kills friends, and erodes the public's confidence in fair play. When a crime is committed in or around your city, town or neighborhood, the community is fraught with suspicion until the perpetrator is apprehended and convicted.

FOR ADULTS ONLY: Specially, THE 6 – 9TH of the TEN COMMANDMENTS are clear, and as given to Moses by GOD, the Commandments are: 6. YOU SHALL NOT MURDER 7. YOU SHALL NOT COMMIT ADULTRY 8. YOU SHALL NOT STEAL 9. YOU SHALL NOT BEAR FALSE WITNESS - If there isn't an error in time- periods, the bible came before The Mayflower in 1492, The Constitution of the United States of America, Democracy, political parties, The Bill or Rights and voting - If the reader can agree that this analysis is correct, then the bible introduced COMMON SENSE before America was established at Plymouth Rock.

Crime has a history on earth as far back as Genesis, whereas IN THE BEGINNING GOD CREATED THE HEAVENS AND THE EARTH, this means that common sense preceded common law!

POLITICS AND CRIME

▲ ▲ ▲

On May 18, 2012, THE DRAKE REPORT was written to ad-dress the mortgage and energy crisis – the report was sent to Mrs. Norma Adams Wade, Editor Nancy Perry Graham, State Senator Royce West, US Senator John Cornyn, Chairman Gary Gensler, and US Representative Eddie B. Johnson. US Senator John Cornyn was the only official that acknowledged receipt of the report, and his reply, dated June 28,2012, explained his position as to why the mortgage and energy crisis existed. The complete report will not be made available; nor shall US Senator Cornyn's response be included in this manuscript – However, copies are available upon request.

The above information is included in this book to show my personal interest in the functions of the American government going back almost eleven (11) years – However, this manuscript is not about me, or trying to become famous! As a matter of fact, my struggles with the topic about politics and crime are outside of my areas of expertise, to wit., if THE ALLEGATIONS related to the President of the United States of America, and the White House Staff, had not become newsworthy, readers would not have heard from me ON POLITICAL ISSUES.

FOR ADULTS ONLY: The time has come to look exclusively at the facts related to allegations about a President, his son, and the family's involvement in bribery. In the same way that fact gathering in a criminal case is investigated, criminologists have an obligation to investigate fully, and honestly all sides of an allegation; but not having the ability to interview witnesses is an impediment! **Thus, what you are about to read in this book is pure speculation based on television reports and the internet.**

As television reports have shown:

1. It is alleged that a top official's son lost a laptop that was given to the FBI in 2018
2. The laptop was given to the FBI by a computer repairman.
3. The computer repairman stated: "he waited for the FBI to contact him."
4. The computer repairman states: from the date he reported the laptop, no FBI contacted him.
5. A witness to the son's participation in the alleged SCANDEL reported that he was in the meeting when the top official attended the same business meeting.
6. The interview with the witness took place on FOX News.
7. The top official's press secretary, at a press conference, said that the top official was not involved, nor had he spoken to his son about his business dealings.
8. The top official's press secretary, in a later press conference, said that the top official was not in business with his son.
9. When the press secretary was challenged about the difference between her two statements, the press secretary said that nothing had changed.

A second witness met with House Republicans and Democrats:

1. A second witness said the top official had been on several calls with his son while his son was involved in selling "THE BRAND."
2. The top official, his son, nor the top official official's family have not been interviewed or subpoenaed.
3. The top official has consistently denied that he was involved in his son's business deals.
4. The top official, on the campaign trail, while engaged in a debate with an opponent, "said that the opponent was involved in receiving money from foreign sources."
5. It is alleged that the top official allowed his son's business partners to visit the White House, while the top official occupied a position in the White House on several occasions.
6. It is also alleged that the top official stated on a television news show, if the prosecutor is not fired, that the country would not receive one billion dollars - He is also reported to have said, after being challenged by an official in that country; who said he could not withhold the funds, because the president of the USA was the one with authority ... the top official, in his response to the challenger, said: " CALL HIM!"...
The TOP OFFICIAL is reported to have said to the officials: that the country had until his flight left to make a decision...The top official then boastfully said, "S.O.B, the prosecutor was fired"!

THE following questions MUST be answered before congress can go forward:
Name the countries that participated, and how much each country paid?

1. UKRAINE = 10 million
2. RUSSIA = 3.5 million
3. KAZAKHSTAN =?
4. CHINA =?
5. ROMANIA =?

What Evidence is lacking or missing:

1. Witnesses from the above listed countries
2. The money trails.
3. Confirmation as to who was paid.
4. How much actual cash did each recipient get.
5. Are offshore accounts holding money?
6. Bank records for each person that received money.

Which agencies were involved in the investigation:

1. Federal Bureau of Investigation - FBI
2. Department of Justice – DOJ
3. Central Intelligence Agency – CIA
4. What were their roles?
5. Did each agency keep records of interviews, etc.?
6. If records were kept, where are the records?

What are the facts that support any/all allegations?

OTHER THAN ALLEGATIONS, THERE IS NO FACTS

TODAY, AUGUST 11, 2023, IT WAS LEARNED THAT THE DEPARTMENT OF JUSTICE APPOINTED A SPECIAL COUNSEL TO PURSUE THE HUNTER BIDEN LEGAL PROBLEM! THE APPOINTMENT OF A SPECIAL COUNSEL TO INVESTIGATE THE BIDEN SCANDAL APPEARS TO BE NOTHING MORE THAN DELAY TACTICS!

What are the alternatives for the President of THE UNITED STATES OF AMERICA today?

1. The President can resign.
2. The President can start a war to remain in office.
3. The President can confess to selling America out!
4. The President can face IMPEACHMENT and hope to survive!
5. The President can stop using DISTRACTIONS to avoid embarrassment.
6. The President MUST admit, one way or the other, about his involvement in Corruption!

America the beautiful has been placed in harm's way by allegations of corruption, or suspicion that the country's President, and his family are not honest! To correct and/or remove the suspicion, that the President is not involved in CORRUPTION – the President must disclose how he made his money to become rich over the past fifty (50) years!

The President MUST also explain how he became wealthy, and how he invested his salary to accomplish becoming a millionaire. The same question MUST be asked of Nancy Pelosi, the former Speaker of the House, to determine how her husband was lucky enough to invest in the MARKET at the right time, so that the Pelosi family could become rich?

FOR ADULTS ONLY: God Bless and forgive those who have forgotten why they were elected to public office – Give America the strength to recover, and get back to love, trust, and honesty. Let democracy come alive in the face of all allegations, or speculations that the author believes will destroy this GREAT NATION. Should America continue down a path of division politically, racially, and in terms of the have's vs the have not's, nothing can save America!

CONSTITUTIONAL ISSUES

▲ ▲ ▲

If The Bill of Rights represents the guiding principle of democracy, why has the current administration taken every opportunity to stall or block the application of the Amendments, except when/where those Amendments protect the Administration from a total investigation. To avoid this manuscript being accused of BIAS, it is important that the Bill of Rights be re-visited. The Bill of Rights are:

1. Congress shall make no law respecting an establishment of religion, or prohibiting the free exercise thereof; or abridging the freedom of speech, or of the press; or the right of the people peaceably to assemble; and to petition the Government for a redress of grievances.
2. A well-regulated militia, being necessary to the security of a free State, the right of the people to keep and bear arms shall not be infringed.
3. No soldier shall, in time of peace be quartered in any house without the consent of the owner; nor in time of war but in a manner to be prescribed by law.
4. The right of the people to be secure in their persons, houses, papers, and effects, against unreasonable searches

and seizures, shall be violated, and no warrant shall issue but upon probable cause, supported by oath or affirmation, and particularly describing the place to be searched, and the persons or things to be seized.

5. **No person shall be held to answer for a capital or otherwise infamous crime, unless on presentment or indictment of a Grand Jury, except in cases arising in the land or naval forces, or in the militia, when in actual service in time of war or public danger; nor shall any person be subject for the same offense to be twice put in jeopardy of life or limb; nor shall be compelled in any criminal case to be a witness against himself, nor be deprived of life, liberty, or property without due process of law; nor shall private property be taken for public use without just compensation.**

6. **In all criminal prosecutions, the accused shall enjoy the right to a speedy and public trial, by an impartial jury of the State and district wherein the crime shall have been committed, which district shall have been previously ascertained by law, and to be informed of the nature and cause of the accusation; to be confronted with witnesses in his favor, and to have the assistance of counsel for his defense.**

7. In suits at common law, where the value in controversy shall exceed twenty dollars, the right of trial by jury shall be preserved, and no fact tried by a jury shall be otherwise re-examined in any court of the United States than according to the rules of common law.

8. **Excessive bail shall not be required, nor excessive fine imposed, nor cruel an unusual punishment inflicted.**

9. The enumeration in the Constitution of certain rights shall not be construed to deny or disparage others retained by the people.

10. The powers not delegated to the United States by the Constitution, nor prohibited by it to the States, are reserved to the States respectively, or to the people.

Post-Civil War Amendments – Amendment 14

No State shall make or enforce any law which shall abridge the privileges or immunities of citizens of the United States, nor shall any State deprive any person of life, liberty, or property, without due process of law; nor deny to any person within its jurisdiction the equal protection of the law.

OBFUSCATION DESTRACTION AND DELUSIONS

▲ ▲ ▲

And God said, "This is the sign of the covenant I am making between me and you and every living creature with you, a covenant of all generations to come: I have set my rainbow in the clouds, and it will be the sign of the covenant between me and the earth."

The book of GENISIS 9: 12-13 INTRODUCES THE WORLD TO THE CONTROL OF JESUS CHRIST – No matter what happens on earth, God is in control – Yet Christians should be allowed to tell the truth about a government that they believe has gone wrong!

It is alleged that the current leadership in America has strayed away from Traditions, Faith, The Constitution, and The Bible. If you will, it is important to know that not all Christians have followed the current leadership in this country – And I am pleased to know and understand that Christians yet exist, not to defy the political leadership, but to glorify God.

FOR ADULTS ONLY: Based on FOX news accounts the current leadership in America, from the President's office to the upper levels of Federal Law enforcement, are corrupt! The mere SUGGESTION/IDEA that the federal government can't be trusted is painful, and dangerous!

Obfuscation, distractions, and delusions take root in a country when citizens believe that their government can't be trusted – citizens that live in a country that they can no longer believe in, will began to take safety measures to protect themselves from criminals, inflation, food shortages, and government leadership – America is in a bad place today - in some States citizens are beginning to understand that the have's vs the have not's is the beginning of Civil War ... NO LAW = NO ORDER!

Criminals cannot be normalized, or changed when they are allowed to steal up to $950 without being apprehended, tried, and convicted for their crime(s) – Criminals earned their name and definition by their illegal acts – Today, all that criminals need is to have enough courage to commit crime(s)! Sooner than later, criminals will transition their criminality, to adding rape, robbery, and murder to force unwilling victims to cooperate!

▲ ▲ ▲

The current political leadership appears to recognize that there are benefits when problems are created, such as, eliminating oil production, opening the Southern Borders, requiring that all drivers purchase an electric vehicle, defunding the police, as well as closing businesses and schools during a crisis.

Using policies and mandates, the upper levels of government are threatening to use the legislature to add Judges to the US Supreme Court; attack our BILL OF RIGHTS, and not liking the First, and Second Amendment says the amendments are a danger to humanity - In addition to these stated threats; politicians, on both sides, are allowing China, Iran, North Korea, and Russia, the latitude and/or permission to hold the United States of America hostage economically.

MARK 10: 42-45, explains what is happing to America, and it reads: Jesus call them to him and saith unto them., "Ye know that they which are accounted to rule over the Gentiles exercise lordship over them, and their high officials exercise authority over them. 43: But so shall it not be among you: but whosoever will be great among you, shall be your minister: 44: And whosoever of you will be chiefest, shall be servant of all. 45: For even the Son of man came not to be ministered unto, but to minister, and to give his life a ransom for many."

It appears that the President of the United States of America, The Department of Justice, The Federal Breau of Investigations, and The Depart of Defense are deciding what the future of this country should be – Democracy should not be defined by politicians, but by the people that politicians represent – The people MUST be subject to the authority of Jesus Christ, a Son of man that paid with his life to save the world. In other words, Power comes from GOD, it was given to Jesus Christ, and was taught to Christians.

FOR ADULTS ONLY: It is not my call to decide what the rest of the world should do, or is doing – And again, it is not the purpose of this book to decide on which political party that you should belong to - But the overall design of this work, and the need for this work is to inform people about what the future holds if nothing changes doing the next election.

It is troubling to see some Americans vote for theft, give free reign to criminals, and condone stupidity, over, and over, and over, again – And it worse to see politicians that will allow criminals to take advantage of people and stores simply to get votes – And even worse is the fact that black politicians are willing to act like oppressors when they allow young blacks to walk into stores and loot!

The greatest problem associated with young criminals is, many don't know or understand that the type of revolution that

is being waged has two ends, prison, and death! As a matter of fact, getting even, or attempting to get revenge for a period in history wherein these young people were not impacted, is dangerous, and in all probability will ultimately cost young criminals greatly!

WHERE HAS CIVILITY GONE

▲ ▲ ▲

(John Stuart Mill, On Liberty, 1859), defined civility in this way: "But the peculiar of evil of silencing the expression of an opinion is that it is robbing the human race, posterity as well as the existing generation – those who dissent from the opinion, still more than those who hold it. If the opinion is right, they are deprived of the opportunity of exchanging error for truth; if wrong, they lose, what is almost as great a benefit, the clearer perception and livelier impression of truth produced by its collision with error."

FOR ADULTS ONLY: Nothing of value can be hidden or concealed from the truth – And nothing is gained by lying to protect oneself or others from scrutiny! Today, the highest levels of government are under suspicion, and it appears that the government, using distractions, is attempting to hide the truth. When leadership at the highest levels come under suspicion for doing wrong, it is incumbent for all Americans to speak up about the problem(s) that are created!

Common Sense is what is needed, about politics, religion, policy, mandates, transgender issues and voting rights. Politicians that profit from voters who support them by buying their vote to gain a "FEW DOLLARS MORE" is unacceptable – Before you hate the messenger, look at your voting record to see if this VOTE BUYING SCHEME describes you!

On August 11, 2023, after learning of a "sweetheart deal" that allowed a federal prosecutor to give special privileges to a government official's son – I became irate because the IRS, DOJ, and others in our government seemingly looked the other way for years, instead of applying the law in a fair and impartial manner – In my opinion, fairness, and honesty, was in essence altogether ignored, and American justice was not served when the DOJ assigned a Special Prosecutor to a case when the son of the president had entered a plea of guilt.

The body of work contained in this manuscript has no political basis or purpose; and it is not the intention of this work to influence thoughts or the law. No names have been used to avoid misinformation, as the writer lives in DeSoto, Texas, not Washington D.C. Regarding the speculation that is to follow, the writer plans to introduce predictions, and analogies to announce where politics will take America in future.

The predictions, and analogies that are to be written are not factual; because as of August 19, 2023, no court or trial date has been assigned to specifically identify any wrongdoing BY the parties.

BUT REMEMBER DEFORE YOU VOTE, TO EXAMINE THE FACTS, UNDERSTAND THE ISSUES CLEARLY, AND IF YOU DON'T KNOW THE FACTS OR ISSUES, DON'T VOTE simply because of the way someone else voted. BUT ABOVE ALL ELSE, DON'T ALLOW ANYONE TO PAY FOR YOUR VOTE!

PREDICTIONS AND ANALYSIS

▲ ▲ ▲

In response to the news that a governmental official's son was going to court, and a plea arrangement had been agreed to by all lawyers; it was believed the judge would sign the plea arrangement, without reading the document. Much to my surprise, the judge denied/delayed the son's plea arrangement, sent both lawyers back to the "drawing board;" with instructions to FIX THE PLEA AGREEMENT!

> **PREDICTION:** Following the judge's orders, the Department of Justice assigned a SPECIAL COUNSEL to the son's case. To further complicate matters, and by design, there are two (2) problems associated with the Department of Justice's delayed action: 1) the delayed action of appointing a Special Counsel will extend, any or all, prosecution of the son. 2) but more troubling is the ISSUE that the same lawyer that orchestrated a "GET-OUT-OF-JAIL- FREE- CARD" for the son, is appointed as Special Counsel by the Department of Justice!

ANALYSIS: Going forward, "WE CANNOT COMMENT, BECAUSE THE ALLEGATIONS ARE UNDER INVESTIGATIONS," Are the beginnings of protecting the son, and the government official from scrutiny, while using the Department of Justice to cover up any alleged crimes!

PREDICTION: The appointment of a Special Counsel is not only a distraction, but has been done by the Department of Justice, to "slow walk" the prosecution of the son, as well as to prevent the investigation from impacting the government official.

ANALYSIS: Rather than subpoena the Special Counsel that has been assigned, The House should demand weekly, televised reports to show, step-by-step, the process and progress of the Special Counsel – To subpoena the Special Counsel would only further delay an investigation into the son, and the government official.

PREDICTION: A note of caution to THE HOUSE OF REPRESENTATIVES - Don't rush to judgements, and don't be so self-assured about the guilt or innocence of the son or the government official until, and unless, the evidence is complete, with documentation supported by bank transfers, the names of any or all recipients of funds that are recorded. Also needed are the names of countries, and amounts of cash that each country sent.

ANALYSIS: The most important feature of this investigation, if possible, would be to bring those persons that can show documented evidence of their contributions – Thereafter, the government official, the head of the Department of Justice, the head of the Federal bureau of Investigations, if the allegations are found in the affirmative, should be impeached.

The former Speaker of the House, Newt Gingrich, A New York Times Bestselling Author said: "…Visuals matter more than words. Style matters more than convention. The overall impression matters more than the details."

COMMON SENSE IS
NOT BASED IN THEORY

▲ ▲ ▲

Common Sense should be the focus of this investigation, not party affiliation, personal experiences, politics, or anything that will move America away from FORGIVENESS. II Corinthians 5:17 states clearly: "Therefore if any man be in CHRIST, HE IS A NEW CREATURE: old things are passed away; behold, all things are become new." 1 John 1:9 says: "If we confess our sins, HE is faithful and just to FORGIVE us our sins, and to cleanse us from all unrighteousness."

FOR CHRISTIAN ADULTS ONLY: Let me admit, that I have not been THE BEST CHRISTIAN in years past; and it is extremely difficult for me to forgive what is suspicioned about the son of a President, the President, Department of Justice, and the Federal bureau of Investigations - According to some news sources, the president as well as other "heads of departments", are criminals! As a Christian, I should not harbor the feeling that are hidden in the recesses of my mind that have a desire to convict the son and impeach the president. And it is difficult for me, as a Christian, to feel the kinds of things that you are reading about here – However At 77 years of age, it is important to understand that I am human;

but as a Christian, it is more important to know that judgement is in GOD'S HANDS: **TO JESUS BE THE GLORY, THE SON OF THE LIVING GOD!**

The above "For Christian Adults Only," is not a confession, but is a realistic assessment which every American should have **before casting a vote** for the LEADER OF THE FREE WORLD. PROVERBS 10:1-2 says:" A wise son makes a glad father, But a foolish son is the grief of his mother. Treasures of wickedness profit nothing, But righteousness delivers from death. The Lord will not allow the righteous soul to famish, But HE casts away the desire of the wicked."

It is incumbent on each American to pray for our nation, our families, and our selves; so that the nation can grow in peace and prosperity – The greatest prayer should be that all who inhabit the earth move closer to GOD, in service to others, love of others, and do this in JESUS' name.

The writing of this book has been a struggle because it was not my intention to write this book at all – And on many occasions I said I would not go on, yet something pushed me to continue writing, with the insistence that the written word would not be hateful, discouraging, or spiteful.

When cleaning my closets, I ran across a book that was sent to me by a family member, Colvin Blanford, Rel.D., the title of the book is GOD FIRST … FOR A BETTER LIFE … BIBLICAL PRINCIPLES FOR BETTER LIVING. The book was sent to my wife, Cynthia, and I on April 30, 2021; because of the book, I feel strongly I can complete this work without being prejudice toward the PRESIDENT OF THE UNITED STATES OF AMERICA.

Pastor Colvin's quote from a time when he was the minister of First Baptist Church in Gary Indiana said: "there was a sign in the junior high classroom that read" …" If you were arrested for being a Christian, would there be enough evidence to convict you?"

Neither am I able to answer that question or take measures to confirm that would qualify me to ask that question of others – But I would miss out on an opportunity to help others, should I not attempt to make a statement about conviction. LUKE 16:11-12 and it reads: **"So if you have not been trustworthy in handling worldly wealth, who will trust you with true riches? And if you have not been trustworthy with someone else's property, who will give you property of your own?**

Common sense explains to all Americans how to conduct themselves in the presence of others, as well as in their private lives. The law was created to reinforce the accepted rules among us and is consistent with what citizens should do. The problem with SHOULD is that not every person will do the right thing(s).

Hebrews 6:11,12,18-20 relates to the author's views about common sense, the scripture says: 11) "And we desire that every one of you do shew the same diligence to the full assurance of hope unto the end:12) That ye be not slothful, but followers of them who through faith and patience inherit the promises. 18) That by two immutable things, in which it was impossible for God to lie, we might have a strong consolidation, who have fled for refuge to lay hold upon the hope set before us: 19) Which hope we have as an anchor of the soul, both sure and stedfast, and which entereth into that within the veil; 20) Whither the forerunner is for us entered, even Jesus, made an high priest for ever after the order of Melchisedec."

Nothing can be hidden from Jesus Christ, Our Lord and Savior, and I am asking those of us who do pay attention to politics, to not participate in listening to political arguments that have no right or wrong answers. Whatever happens in future, I think that God will have the last word - The president, Congress, and Judges will control issues that occur on earth, but God will have command of the entire universe, and HE will dispense a final justice!

For clarification, it is important that the Advisors to the President of the United States of America, tell him that he is not exempt from God's mercy, and forgiveness – and it would be wise to admit his participation, if any, in unlawfulness and/or questionable conduct that was used to enrich his family.

From where I sit, and based on some news services accounts, the President has used distractions to cover up the legal issues that have a potential to destroy the country, his family, and the laws that are designed to keep America strong.

A DIVIDED AMERICA

▲ ▲ ▲

Much like the Civil War America is again divided, ironically, the same two (2) political parties are involved; Democrats and Republicans – However the new divisions are the result of differences of opinion related to power grabs, money, the border, inflation, race relations, and the struggles between Republicans in the House of Representatives, and the President of the United States of America about IMPEACHMENT!

Using distractions, the president appears to leverage decisions that negatively impact average citizens with limited incomes. The strategy for leveraging decisions by the president appears to be a method to "slow walk" investigations into the activities of his son, and the president himself.

FOR ADULTS ONLY: This part of my book is certain to anger some citizens, in that from Desoto, Texas, a person who lives outside of Washington D.C., is evaluating the President of the United States of America using a job performance evaluation - There is but one response to those that will disagree with the job performance evaluation of the president, and that response is: PRAY for me, as well as the president! Others that read this book will ask how does a "nobody" from Texas think that he is qualified to evaluate the president. The answer to that question is: I am a citizen of the

United States of America, as a citizen, I have the right to evaluate the service of an elected official because The Constitution of United States of America allows me to vote...**ENOUGH SAID**

- OVERALL, JOB PERFORMANCE

- ACCOMPLISHMENTS

- KNOWS JOB REQUIREMENTS

- ACTS RESPONSIBLY

- IS TRUSTWORTHY

- ALWAYS ON TIME

- PROMPT

- RESPECTS OTHERS

- IS RELIABLE

- FREQUENTLY LATE TO WORK

- EXCEEDS MAXIMUM VACATION TIME

- DOES NOT RESPECT OTHERS

SUPRIZE! This work will not attempt to complete the actual job performance of the president, that job will be left to readers of this book, much like the author, you too have the right to vote – which means that your judgement about the performance of the president, as his employer, is required.

Before evaluating the job performance of the president, make sure, as the evaluator (past or present), that you could get a raise for your job performance.

THE PREDICTIONS FOR AMERICA

▲ ▲ ▲

What do I know, and how do I know what the future holds for America? If crime is not stopped, criminals will continue to boldly engage in criminal acts. **CRIME IS A PRELUDE TO WAR!** As can be seen in California, and New York, crime has escalated. In Dallas, Texas, criminals are watching to see what other criminals are doing in major cities – Criminals in Dallas, Texas, should be aware that California, and New York, are very different from Texas – Texans are allowed to defend themselves, and others from criminal activity.

A word of caution to criminals that are watching television in Texas: DON'T ATTEMPT TO ROB, RAPE, STEAL, or MURDER. In other words, please don't bet your life that Texans will go along with the kinds of criminal activities that take place in California, New York, Chicago, Philadelphia, and Baltimore. **ENOUGH SAID**

ECCLESIASTES 2:22-26 explains that even work can be harmful when it is overdone, the scripture reads: "What does a man get for all the toil and anxious striving with which he labors under the sun? All his days his work is pain and grief; even at night his mind does not rest … A man can do nothing better than to eat and drink and find satisfaction in his work. This too, I see, is from the hand of God …To the man who pleases him, God gives wisdom, knowledge, and happiness."

Criminals face an additional responsibility, the stress of avoiding law enforcement, jail, and prison. The new wave of crime, groups committing crimes, is a threat to the safety of all Americans!

CRIME HAS TO STOP, OR, BE STOPPED

WHERE HAS THE AMERICAN SPIRIT GONE

▲ ▲ ▲

Some years ago, growing up poor was looked upon and ignored because every person that lived in South Terrell, Texas, was poor. In the "hood" where I grew up, only one person had a football, and not allowing that individual to play on a team meant the person who owned the football would threaten to take his ball and go home – If the owner took the ball and left the playground, the football game could not be played!

Ironically, it appears that politically, some Americans have decided to destroy the Constitution, the Declaration of Independence, the Bill of Rights, the Bible, and remove common sense and objective thinking out of the hands of citizens. These same politicians are attempting, using the power granted via elections, to manipulate and destroy anyone who opposes their ideology.

In some cases, it appears that prosecutors are taking a position to allow crime(s) to go unpunished because of race. A few States, when race is introduced as a causative factor, either don't permit arrest, or they don't prosecute transgressor's – In these same States, prosecutors and politicians are re-elected because of their position on defunding the police.

At the highest levels of our government, politicians use their office for an opportunity to become wealthy – when these politicians leave office, they don't retire in the traditional sense; many are hired by companies as lobbyist, or they are employed by colleges, and other institutions where they become even richer.

Not being a Court of Law, or a lawyer, restricts what can be said or written about individual cases; and the names of individuals not yet convicted of a crime, should not, and cannot be stated in the affirmative as to their guilt or innocence – And very carefully, and unless a person pleads guilty or is found guilty of an offense, this book has avoided using names, dates, or places where a crime is alleged to have happened.

What can be said or investigated is to ask: "where has the American spirit gone," why has our country been taken hostage by politicians, and what will happen to America, if someone doesn't get a pair … And retake the American Spirit! Why can't criminals be punished for all levels of criminal activity, why does losing a job count as punishment at certain levels for crime(s) that are committed?

To be honest, I can't answer any of the above questions, and I shouldn't be asked to provide more than my opinion as to why there is concern related to "the Spirit of America." But I will take a shot at answering the questions with one phrase … America no longer trust or believes in traditions or each other – And most Americans are "bullied" to shut them up!

▲ ▲ ▲

Muriel Solomon, in the book "WHAT DO I SAY WHEN…" explains:" how to deal with bullies, and how to counterpunch;" the expressions, although not related to politics specifically, are needed when confronting critics – this is especially true when dealing with political appointees who are not elected, but use their power to control, or limit the control of others! Solomon says: "Be still for a couple of minutes and let the bully land those cutting remarks without interrupting. Force yourself to wear a pleasant I know something you don't know expression while you prepare your response. Now get in the ring, even if your bully hasn't stopped jabbing."

THANK YOU, AND GOD BLESS YOU
FOR READING THIS BOOK

Milton Keynes UK
Ingram Content Group UK Ltd.
UKHW022353221123
433027UK00004B/88

9 798822 928640